On Set

Written by
Daisy Hawkins

Illustrated by
Pablo Gallego

Bill is on set.

Tess is on set.

3 ... 2 ... 1 ... Go!

Tess pips Bill, log to log.

Bill is not hot
on the log run.

Tess tucks up to fit
in the gap.

Can Bill?

Tess ducks and
can miss the mud.

Bill did not duck.
Bill fell in the mud.

Can Tess get to the top of the big red hill?

Can Bill?

Bill and Tess on set.